Date: 9/30/16

APRIL FOOLS' DAY WHAT A JOKE!

BY THEODORE JONES

Gareth Stevens
PUBLISHING

Please visit our website, www.garethstevens.com. For a free color catalog of all our high-quality books, call toll free 1-800-542-2595 or fax 1-877-542-2596.

Library of Congress Cataloging-in-Publication Data

Jones, Theodore (Theodore Francis), 1978-
 April Fools' Day : what a joke! / Theodore Jones.
    pages cm. — (The history of our holidays)
 Includes bibliographical references and index.
ISBN 978-1-4824-3882-6 (pbk.)
ISBN 978-1-4824-3883-3 (6 pack)
ISBN 978-1-4824-3884-0 (library binding)
1. April Fools' Day—Juvenile literature. I. Title.
 GT4995.A6J66 2016
 394.262—dc23
                                   2015018190

Published in 2016 by
Gareth Stevens Publishing
111 East 14th Street, Suite 349
New York, NY 10003

Copyright © 2016 Gareth Stevens Publishing

Designer: Sarah Liddell
Editor: Therese Shea

Photo credits: Cover, p. 1 (main) Kitto Studio/Shutterstock.com; cover, p. 1 (whoopee cushion) Mega Pixel/Shutterstock.com; background texture throughout secondcorner/Shutterstock.com; background flags throughout saicle/Shutterstock.com; p. 5 Pressmaster/Shutterstock.com; p. 7 Marzolino/Shutterstock.com; p. 9 Artur Debat/Moment/Getty Images; p. 11 (penguins) Wikipedia/Mbz1; p. 11 (elephants) ullstein bild/Contributor/ullstein bild/Getty Images; p. 13 wavebreakmedia/Shutterstock.com; p. 14 Wikimedia Commons/Gilbertus; p. 15 Karl Gehring/Contributor/Denver Post/Getty Images; p. 17 Gang Liu/Shutterstock.com; p. 19 nito/Shutterstock.com; p. 21 agusyonok/Shutterstock.com.

Printed in the United States of America

CPSIA compliance information: Batch #CW16GS: For further information contact Gareth Stevens, New York, New York at 1-800-542-2595.

CONTENTS

Boldface words appear in the glossary.

A Tricky Day

Has anyone ever played a trick on you on April 1? April Fools' Day is a holiday all about playing tricks that's **celebrated** around the world. How did such a strange day come about? There are lots of guesses.

5

Hilaria

April Fools' Day has been celebrated for **centuries**. It's a lot like some **ancient** holidays. For example, the Romans celebrated a day called Hilaria on March 25. On this day, Romans pretended to be other people.

7

Holi

The celebration of Holi takes place in northern India in the spring during a full moon. People play tricks and throw colored water and **powder** on each other. Then, they wash it off and put on white clothes.

9

Pranks and Jokes

No matter how the day got started, April Fools' Day has become a day of **pranks** around the world. Newspapers, TV, and websites use fake photos and news to trick people. One news show pretended they found a group of flying penguins!

Some tricks are simple, such as telling a story that isn't true. Others are actions, like tying someone's shoes together. This could be dangerous! The best April Fools' Day jokes aren't mean and don't hurt people.

Some tricks are **complicated**. Do you see the cake on the next page? It's actually a roll of paper towels that's been cut and frosted—just like a cake! This **subway** car was made to look like it crashed into the street!

15

Around the World

In Scotland, April Fools' Day is called Gowkie Day. A gowk (GOWK) is another name for a **cuckoo**. It's also a word for a foolish person. In Scotland, people may put a sign on someone's back that says: "Kick me!"

In France, the person who's fooled is called *poisson d'avril* (pwah-SOHN dah-VREEL), which means "April fish." This probably means a fish that's easily caught. French children may put a paper fish on someone's back on April Fools' Day.

In the Ukraine, people dress up and march in a big parade. Some people even sell jokes! Wherever you are on April Fools' Day, make sure you don't get tricked. And if you're doing the tricking, don't forget to yell, "April Fools!"

21

GLOSSARY

ancient: belonging to a time that was long ago

celebrate: to honor with special activities

century: 100 years

complicated: having many parts or steps

cuckoo: a bird that lays its eggs in the nests of other birds and has a call like its name

powder: matter in the form of very small bits

prank: a trick or joke done for fun

subway: a system of underground trains in a city

FOR MORE INFORMATION

BOOKS

Dolphin, Colleen. *April Fools' Day to Z Day: Holidays from A to Z*. Edina, MN: ABDO Publishing, 2009.

LaRoche, Amelia. *April Fool's Day Jokes to Tickle Your Funny Bone*. Berkeley Heights, NJ: Enslow Publishers, 2013.

WEBSITES

April Fools Tradition Popularized

www.history.com/this-day-in-history/ april-fools-tradition-popularized
Read some of the famous pranks that have been pulled on this funny holiday.

Where Does April Fools' Day Originate?

news.discovery.com/history/ origins-of-april-fools-day-20130401.htm
Discover more about where this holiday may come from.

INDEX